Rethinking Christmas

Rethinking Christmas

Poems for Advent and Christmas

S T Kimbrough, Jr.

Foreword by James H. Charlesworth
Preface by Timothy E. Kimbrough

RESOURCE *Publications* • Eugene, Oregon

RETHINKING CHRISTMAS
Poems for Advent and Christmas

Copyright © 2020 S T Kimbrough, Jr. All rights reserved. Except for brief quotations in critical publications or reviews, no part of this book may be reproduced in any manner without prior written permission from the publisher. Write: Permissions, Wipf and Stock Publishers, 199 W. 8th Ave., Suite 3, Eugene, OR 97401.

Resource Publications
An Imprint of Wipf and Stock Publishers
199 W. 8th Ave., Suite 3
Eugene, OR 97401

www.wipfandstock.com

PAPERBACK ISBN: 978-1-7252-7283-5
HARDCOVER ISBN: 978-1-7252-7282-8
EBOOK ISBN: 978-1-7252-7284-2

Manufactured in the U.S.A.   06/11/20

Contents

Foreword by James H. Charlesworth — vii
Preface by Timothy E. Kimbrough — xi
Introduction — xiii

Section 1: Before Christ Comes

1. Give Thanks Before Advent — 2
2. Advent Expectation — 3
3. Awaiting Advent — 4
4. The Advent Plea — 5
5. The Advent Quest — 6
6. Advent—Repent — 7
7. God's Countenance — 8
8. Love Before Bethlehem? — 9

Section 2: When Christ Comes

9. Angels' Song — 12
10. Theotokos, Mother of God — 13
11. Mary's Lullaby — 15
12. Mary, Joseph, Shepherds, Kings — 17
13. Child of Peace — 19
14. Christmas Time is Here at Last — 21
15. God's Homeless Child — 23
16. Who Was He? — 25
17. Emmanuel—God with Us — 26

Section 3: After Christ Comes

18. O, Jesus Child, Where are You?	28
19. Mourning for Bethlehem	29
20. The Christmas Bells of Bethlehem	31
21. The Bethlehem Wall	32
22. Questions and Answers	34
23. The Holy Grail of Christmas	35
24. Corporate Christmas Cheer	37
25. Time to Cheer	38
26. Christmas Carols	39

Section 4: Until Christ Comes

27. Nothing New Under the Sun?	42
28. Who Is An Angel?	44
29. Whose Child Is This?	45
30. We Pray for Peace	47
31. Rethinking Christmas	48
32. Seeing the Unseen	49
33. Christmas Joy	51
34. Joy	52
35. A Single Bell	53
36. No Christmas is the Same	54
37. Christmas Memories	55
38. Too Late for Peace, Goodwill?	56
39. If Christmas Comes	57
40. Give Peace, Goodwill New Birth	59

Foreword

Feeling the Wonder of God's New Message for Us

In April of the year 30, Jesus's followers gathered in Jerusalem. Many came from Nazareth, Migdal, and Capernaum. Some had witnessed Jesus's arrest, pondered his crucifixion, and were convinced that God had raised him from the dead. Many had even seen their risen Lord. They crafted an Aramaic affirmation that is embedded in the Greek New Testament: *maran atha*: "Our Lord has arrived" (found in 1 Corinthians 16:22; cf. *Didache* 10:14).

These believers descended from Jews who had waited for centuries for God's saving action. They yearned for the Messiah to be sent by God to bring the power of David and the wisdom of Solomon back to the nation God had chosen. All faithful Jews knew God's promise recorded in the Hebrew Scriptures (the Old Testament).

Gathering in the Temple and all over the Holy Land, vast numbers of Jews believed that God had heard – finally – the cries of his people. They knew God heard the pleas during the invasion of the Assyrians, Babylonians, and Persians. God had answered Jewish prayers during the invasion of Alexander the Great and the Greeks, Parthians, and Romans. They were enthused by the successes of the Maccabees and the restoration of Temple worship.

Followers of Jesus believed — they claimed to know — that God had broken his silence, announced through a dove (as with Noah) that redemption was nigh. God had spoken through the truly human Jesus. God's resurrection powers proved Good News must be shared throughout the world. A Pharisee who once hated these believers became "the

Apostle of the Gentiles." He refused to be stopped or slowed; he advanced forward, enduring severe punishments, to proclaim the Good News to the West. This eloquent preacher wrote the Epistle to the Romans and other brilliant epistles.

The author of the earliest Christian Hymnbook, the *Odes of Solomon*, penned his thrill at the advent of the Messiah.

> My joy is the Lord and my course is towards Him.
> This way of mine is beautiful.
> For there is a Helper for me, the Lord.
> He has generously shown Himself to me in His simplicity,
> Because His kindness has diminished His grandeur.
>
> He became like me, that I might receive Him.
> In form He was considered like me, that I might put Him on.
>
> And I trembled not when I saw Him,
> Because He was gracious to me.
>
> Like my nature He became, that I might understand Him,
> And like my form, that I might not turn from Him.[1]

Now, with his moving well-crafted poems S T Kimbrough invites us, in our ways and in our own time, to feel the excitement of those first believers in Judea and Galilee. Christians are those who believe that Jesus is the Christ whose Advent Palestinian Jews for centuries had been yearning; and they freely explain their faith in myriads of ways. They are filled with JOY at Advent, Christmas time, when the eyes of old men and women sparkle as they once did as young children on Christmas morn, clambering down stairs to stare with wonder at a sight never imagined.

Advent embodies our JOY. S T Kimbrough helps us feel the magic of those first believers who were inebriated with overflowing wonder and awe. Some believing Jews prayed *marana tha*, "Our Lord, come (back)." From about the year 30 to the late sixties, James, Jesus's brother

---

1. Ode 7:2–6, in J. H. Charlesworth, *The Earliest Christian Hymnbook* (Eugene, OR: Cascade Books, 2009), 17.

Foreword

prayed that prayer in the eastern sections of the Temple, looking eastward and at the Mount of Olives, expecting to see the return of the Son of God, as promised in the Book of Acts.

J. H. Charlesworth
President, Foundation on Judaism and Christian Origins
Editor, Princeton Dead Sea Scrolls Project
George L. Collard Professor of New Testament Emeritus
Princeton Theological Seminary

Preface

As I compose this preface for *Rethinking Christmas,* the world is caught up in the throes of the Coronavirus pandemic and is paralyzed. Only slowly is it beginning to realize a certain loss of innocence. Christians will find a way to hope. Christians will declare that God is Sovereign, and that God will not abandon the people Christ came to save. Nevertheless, the return to any kind of life "as we know it" is far off and will require hard work and imagination on the part of many.

Hard work and imagination are exactly what Dr. Kimbrough asks of the reader in this volume. Although he is an academic, a linguistic scholar, a Charles Wesley expert, and a professional musician, none of these disciplines are brought to bear specifically in this work. Wearing the mantle of poet, he resists the temptation to *deconstruct* Christmas as either cultural icon or cultic reality. Instead, he provides the reader with poems to stretch the heart and mind, soul and conscience.

Taken as a whole, these poems provide a commentary on the Scripture that narrates the birth of the Messiah. They offer the reader a devotional guide through the days and weeks of Advent and Christmas, and even into the anticipated end of the age. The poems also teach. They provide catechesis for the one who would know more about Christ's first coming and its implications for the life of the world. If you read deep into this work, then you will also come to appreciate how the poet's muse serves as prophetic utterance. The beauty and determination of the Messiah's Nativity required the bended knee of shepherds, kings, and angels. As a result, there can be no power or principality of any age that refuses obeisance to the Prince of

Rethinking Christmas

Peace without consequence. See here the application the author makes to the current and ongoing crisis in the Middle East, particularly with regard to the plight of the Palestinians.

As proof that abstraction as a means of reformation was never his goal, Dr. Kimbrough often visits the memory of Christmases past as they unfolded in his life over the last eight decades. The poet's heart is re-shaped and re-molded as he *rethinks* the Christmas observances of his youth and young adulthood. Nevertheless, he resists the lure of nostalgia. A rethought Christmas will not be a warmed-over, sentimental, reconstituted semblance of long-lost celebrations. A rethought Christmas will not assert traditionalist notions of how the season *ought* to be celebrated.

A rethought Christmas, as presented here, will inspire, convict, convert, and lead the reader ever more deeply into the mystery that is the Incarnation of Jesus Christ, the Son of God.

If you dare to open these pages, you must be prepared to work hard, to shed pre-conceived notions of holy-day, and to open your heart to the imagination of God. There may be moments when you are unsettled by what you read. But the reward of the diligent will be a faith renewed.

Timothy E. Kimbrough
Dean of Christ Church Cathedral
Nashville, TN
March 28, 2020
Gregory, the Illuminator, c. 332

Introduction

For many church traditions in the West, Advent begins on the fourth Sunday before Christmas, and Advent marks the beginning of the church year. In Eastern Orthodoxy, however, Advent refers to the forty-day Nativity Fast. Though the observances of western and eastern churches are different, the one thing they have in common is the anticipation of Christ's coming.

The "coming of Christ" (the Greek name is *Christos*) is, of course associated very closely with the birth of Jesus (from the Hebrew name *Yeshu'a*) in the town of Bethlehem. Also, it is intimately bound to the concept of the Advent of Christ within the believer and anticipation of the Second Coming of Christ.

The secularization of Advent and Christmas adds considerable layers of interpretation to what the "coming of Christ" means. To be sure, some of these layers are cultural, as one might expect. In the West, it is fair to say that specific colors, particularly red and green, are associated with these seasons. Churches adorn their naves and altars with greenery, and perhaps poinsettias, and many will add Christmas trees, large and small, often decorated with symbols of the Christian faith.

In addition, one may find a crèche placed at an appropriate place in a church or home with images of the Holy Family and other persons (shepherds, wise men) in the Christmas story. Sometimes animals (sheep, oxen, cattle) fitting to a scene within a stall or cave are also displayed. Hence, the story is humanized, one might say, as Mary, Joseph, the Christ Child, and others appear in visible images.

Rethinking Christmas

At the beginning of each poem in this collection there are quotations of biblical verses from the New Revised Standard Version. Sometimes they are directly related to the following poem. At other times they are affirmations that reflect the continuity between the biblical affirmation and/or theme and the imagination of the poem. For example, prior to the poem "Awaiting Advent" one reads Psalm 37:7, "Be still before the Lord, and wait patiently for him." Clearly, one does not think of this Psalm text as directly related to Advent, yet it is precisely the spirit of the psalmist's affirmation that anticipates one's posture before and during Advent.

In the poems that appear here imagination plays a significant role. We do not know exactly what people expect or anticipate at Advent, but we know it can be radically different, depending on one's situation in life: the poor, the homeless, those enveloped in war, the wealthy, the desperately ill or injured. What one awaits does not change the nature of Christ's coming, but it greatly influences how Christ is received. One thing is quite clear: it is the love of God that descends to earth in this child, a child of peace and goodwill. If one is not awaiting these things, one's celebration may be well-meaning but very wrong-headed.

These poems imagine what Advent and Christmas are not and what they might be. How might they be seen through the eyes of the poor and marginalized? How might they be viewed by a business concern? How are they misunderstood? What does Christmas mean, when a bell rings on Christmas Day, and a church building has been destroyed and all that remains is the bell tower?

What do Advent and Christmas mean when one celebrates them for the first time without a family member who died during the year?

So, I often let my imagination tell the story or an aspect of it. For example, in "Mary's Lullaby" I imagine what Mother Mary might have sung to the Christ Child as an infant. At other times I try to adhere more closely to the narrative of Christ's birth.

As one rethinks the meaning of Advent and Christmas, there are many questions to be entertained. If love came down at Christmas, was there no love among people before Jesus's birth? ("Love Before Bethlehem?") One must ask,

> Did no one speak a loving word?
> Was life of love devoid?
> Could life on earth be that absurd?
> All born to love avoid?

Introduction

As we ask such questions, we realize the importance of seeing Advent as a time of personal examination and reflection. There are very many questions which Advent precipitates, and, if we are honest with ourselves, we will face them honestly and sincerely.

> We ask ourselves would we be wise
>   and seek Emmanuel,
> the humble and the poor then prize
>   with whom love comes to dwell?
> ...
> At Advent, all must take the time
>   to seek an inner peace,
> for inner peace will surely prime
>   one's soul for love's release.

The process of self-examination at Advent should punctuate the reality that as valid as we may think the Christmas message is for all times and all people, peace and goodwill have not overcome the earth, which is filled with hatred and dissension. Hence, Advent should also be a time that calls us to repent for the failure to realize the hopes of the coming of the Christ Child.

> At Advent, thus we must repent
>   that peace, goodwill, are not fulfilled.
> There are no reasons to relent,
>   when hate, divisions are not stilled.
> Let others' guilt be no excuse,
>   though we might cast on them the blame.
> Repent we must for our abuse,
>   for Advent calls us all by name.

The Christmas story raises questions about the identity of the Child born in a stable. The prophets of Israel anticipate the coming of a Messiah and Prince of Peace. To people of faith he is both of these. But clearly in the biblical story he is also a homeless child. Mary and Joseph can find no suitable place in Bethlehem for him to be born. Thus, Mary gives birth in an animal stall.

> There was no place to lay his head,
> a mother's arms his only bed.
> There was no place to birth her boy,
> yet angels hailed his birth with joy.

One cannot escape drawing parallels between Bethlehem at the time of Jesus's birth and Bethlehem today. The town where the Child of peace and goodwill was born is now surrounded by a giant wall, a symbol of division and enmity.

> The Christmas bells of Bethlehem
> ring out "goodwill to all!"
> No matter what one's faith or creed,
> goodwill creates no wall.

"What an illusion that a wall / security and peace can bring." Not far away from Bethlehem today, a home may be destroyed by a rocket, bomb, or bulldozer—hardly an image of peace and goodwill.

There are other barriers to the meaning of Advent and Christmas besides a physical wall. Each year one hears of things that diminish what these seasons should mean. The "ultimate gift of the Christ Child" is remembered symbolically in gifts people give to one another at Christmas. Yet, commercialization and the gifts themselves often seem more important than the "ultimate gift." Hence, one asks

> Can Christmas really take place
> when no gifts have been bought?
> Can Christmas really take place
> when shopping is for naught?

By no means, however, should we fear the joy and celebration of Advent and Christmas.

Introduction

One of the names of this Child is Emmanuel, God with us. Christians hear this name year in and year out, and its meaning is a joyous thing that calls for celebration! This is why we decorate our homes, offices, and churches. This is why mothers, fathers, and friends bake their favorite holiday recipes.

> Colors, smells now tell us all,
> It's time to sing "Deck the hall . . ."
> Christmas time is finally here,
> Happiest time from year to year.

Nevertheless, we cannot forget those who find it difficult to celebrate: the desperately ill, the wounded, the poverty-stricken, the emotionally disturbed. Even so, the celebration and joy the Christ Child brings center not in gifts, decorations, or holiday cuisine. All people, be they rich or poor, healthy or infirmed, rejoice over the same thing: the gift of love in this child who comes to show us the way of peace and goodwill.

> Mary, Joseph, shepherds, kings,
> as the angel chorus sings,
> learn the truth of this Child's birth:
> spread goodwill and peace on earth.

The Christmas story is filled with metaphors, images, and figures that can model for us our own behavior. This can be precarious, if we make false assumptions about what it means to shape our demeanor after Mary, Joseph, shepherds, or wise men. But we may find an image or images we wish to reflect in our behavior. What if the posture of the angels could shape who we are? And we could

> Be guardian angels, never cease
> benevolence, goodwill;
> be watchful guardians of peace,
> for angels do no ill.

Rethinking Christmas

What if each time we see an angel ornament on a Christmas tree, we could see in ourselves the posture of one who proclaims peace and goodwill to others? What if we could see in every child the image of the Christ Child yearning for the love of others? What if a star with its glistening beams of light could symbolize an openness to be willing to touch the lives of others, just as the star sheds light on all in its path?

These poems reflect how we may imagine what Advent and Christmas mean. They are arranged in four sections: 1. Before Christ Comes, 2. When Christ Comes, 3. After Christ Comes, and 4. Until Christ Comes. In the first section the poems address the anticipation of the coming of Christ, especially what precipitates this anticipation in the light of biblical prophecy and the New Testament Gospels. The poems of section two speak specifically to the meaning of the coming of Christ. What transpired after his coming is the question raised in many of the poems of section three, i.e. what transpired in his world and in ours. Section four raises many eschatological questions concerning how Christ's message and life are fulfilled and yet to be fulfilled in our lives and in the future.

Perhaps these poems will encourage you to imagine what Advent and Christmas can mean to you. Do not be afraid to imagine! This does not mean to distort the biblical story, rather to imagine what it means to you and others now. Advent and Christmas are seasons of the imagination of God. The coming of the Christ Child imagines a world of peace and goodwill.

S T Kimbrough, Jr.

Section 1

Before Christ Comes

Revelation 7:12, "Blessing and glory and wisdom
and thanksgiving and honor
and power and might
be to our God forever and ever!"

1. Give Thanks Before Advent

How interesting Thanksgiving Day[1]
    precedes the time Advent:
A day the nation is to pray—
    give thanks is the intent.

Thanksgiving Day's no holy day
    within the Christian year,
and yet before Advent to pray
    brings expectation near.

When thanks and wonder shape our thought
    throughout the Advent time,
through expectation we are taught
    God's love-born paradigm.

---

1. Thanksgiving Day is a national day of thanks in the U.S.A. and occurs on the fourth Thursday of November.

*Galatians 4:4–5, "But when the fullness of time had come,
God sent forth his Son, born of a woman, born under the law,
. . . so that we might receive adoption as children."*

2. Advent Expectation

With Advent, soon to come this year,
    will I expectant be?
Is all that I expect reindeer,
    St. Nick, a Christmas tree?
They've been a part of Advent time
    since I was very young,
along with carols, Christmas rhyme
    that we have always sung.

The atmosphere of Christmas wreathes
    we hang upon our doors,
the sweet aromas each one breathes
    make pleasant Christmas chores.
And yet, is this what I await
    when Advent time is near?
Is this not simply worldly fate
    that transforms Christmas cheer?

At Advent what should I expect?
    a tinseled holiday
or the magnificent prospect
    of love come down to stay?
God's love is what I will await
    that in a child is born,
a love that never comes too late
    on every Christmas morn.

Psalms 37:7, "Be still before the Lord, and wait patiently for him."

3. Awaiting Advent

At Advent what shall we await?
    Glad tidings that a Savior comes?
Is this what we anticipate
    in nations of the world, in homes?

Is this mere fantasy or truth?
    What shall we of this story make,
that we have heard throughout our youth,
    yet, some believe to be a fake?

One thing the story says is true:
    the hope for goodwill and for peace
we must forever keep in view.
    The hope for both must never cease.

The Child of whom the angels sing
    grew up an advocate of peace,
for others gave up everything
    that love among us might increase.

This is the Child we celebrate
    at Advent, take it as you may.
His message: love and peace, not hate,
    a Savior's message still today.

Leviticus 19:18, "You shall love your neighbor as yourself."

4. The Advent Plea

Let Advent hope open the heart
    Messiah's love now to receive,
love's miracle to live each day,
    the Advent miracle believe.

But transform first our saddened thoughts,
    our sadness transform into joy.
Take fear away, reluctant doubt,
    and turn us all to love's employ.

Love's miracle we cannot know
    when we mistreat a foe or friend.
We know it not when love's not shared,
    or we love's miracle misspend.

If we in love would dare believe,
    love's miracle we then must be:
be lovers of the loved, unloved.
    This is the lasting Advent plea.

The Advent story tells of love,
    the love of God for humankind.
It's unconditional for all,
    each person is for love designed.

Psalms 139:23, "Search me, O God, and know my heart; test me and know my thoughts."

5. The Advent Quest

At Advent time, we look within
    with honesty sincere,
to seek the spirit that's akin
    to love devoid of fear.

We ask ourselves would we be wise
    and seek Emmanuel,
the humble and the poor then prize
    with whom love comes to dwell?

Will we make no room in the heart,
    like no room in the inn?
And God's own Love-Child keep apart
    from deepest thoughts within?

At Advent, all must take the time
    to seek an inner peace,
for inner peace will surely prime
    one's soul for love's release.

Matthew 3:2, "Repent, for the kingdom of heaven has come near."

6. Advent—Repent

With centuries past since Christ was born,
    and neither peace nor goodwill reign,
the homeless still remain forlorn,
    and politicians goodwill feign.
Shall we, who now remain on earth,
    repent for these forgotten aims,
which were the purpose of his birth,
    while enemies the other blames.

Claim Christ as Savior, if you will,
    but you may not ignore these goals;
each Advent they are with us still,
    spanning the northern/southern poles.
Even if you for them advocate,
    repentance you cannot ignore.
Your conscience you cannot placate;
    inaction you have tried before.

At Advent, thus we must repent
    that peace, goodwill, are not fulfilled.
There are no reasons to relent,
    when hate, divisions are not stilled.
Let others' guilt be no excuse,
    though we might cast on them the blame.
Repent we must for our abuse,
    for Advent calls us all by name.

Numbers 6:26, "The Lord lift up his countenance upon you, and give you peace."

7. God's Countenance

What makes the Advent season seem
    that it's too short a time?
The days fly past, we can't redeem
    the reason or the rhyme.

We hear the carols, gifts we buy
    but often we don't think
of reasons that reveal the why
    we from the truth may shrink.

It's easy to romanticize
    the gifts that East-kings bring,
and this is the commercial guise
    in stores where carols ring.

Now it is Advent-tide again,
    and now I have the chance,
its deepest meaning to obtain:
    Christ's love, God's countenance.

Now in the Christ-child born anew
    we see the heavenly light;
God's love is there for us to view,
    born on a starlit night.

Job 10:12, "You have granted me life and steadfast love, and your care has preserved my spirit."

8. Love Before Bethlehem?

It's often claimed that love was born
    in Bethlehem of old.
Was then the world of love forlorn?
    Is such a thought too bold?
Did no one speak a loving word?
    Was life of love devoid?
Could life on earth be that absurd:
    all born to love avoid?

Most languages include a word
    that most would say love means;
but explanations I have heard
    seem written by machines.
What kind of love was born that night
    when angels sang of peace?
A love that reaches a new height,
    a love born to increase.

This love that gives of self for all
    is born in a small Child,
who grew to show the great and small,
    none are from love exiled.
When Christ's love dies, he shows us how
    to make love real for all.
Hence, following him we take a vow
    to love whate'er befall.

This means in every circumstance
    our love will live and die
by faith for others, not by chance,
    for Christ has shown us why.
The love that lives is love that dies
    to ego, self, and pride,
seeks giving hearts without disguise
    and nothing else beside.

If Bethl'hem's Child this love did bring
    why cannot I now see—
I with the angels too should sing,
    for love was shown to me.
Self-giving love was in the world;
    it simply did not see:
the thoughts of love that through it swirled
    Christ made reality.

Section 2

When Christ Comes

Luke 2:13, "And suddenly there was with the angel a multitude of the heavenly host, praising God and saying,
'Glory to God in the highest heaven,
and on earth peace, goodwill toward all.'"[2]

9. Angels' Song

Angels sing to hail Christ's birth,
music heard throughout the earth.
It repeats the glad refrain:
Peace, goodwill in him will reign.

He will show that love can heal
when divisions seem so real.
His love's tender and can teach
us to change our hateful speech.

How can one Child do all this?
Help the world see it's remiss
if love does not always reign
in each artery and vein.

This love gives in sacrifice,
asks no payment, has no price.
Love is our Emmanuel,
God with us, joyous Noel!

---

2. The New Revised Standard Version reads: "among those whom he favors."

Acts 1:14, "All these were constantly devoting themselves to prayer, together with certain women, including Mary the mother of Jesus, as well as his brothers."

10. Theotokos,[3] Mother of God

Theotokos, Mother of God,
does this name for Mary seem odd?
The mother of Jesus, God's Son,
explained by the Scriptures is done.
This Mystery begins long ago,
when wisdom divine, folk forego.
It seems so unreal to be true,
a story some see without clue.
An angel announces his birth,
when born, angels sing round the earth,
that this Child brings goodwill and peace
with love that no power can decrease.
Theotokos watches him grow,
but Mary, his mother, can't know
what suffering his peace-love will bring,
or how it will urge souls to sing.
The Mystery beyond us comes down
to Bethlehem's hill-nestled town.
Theotokos, there when he's born;
Theotokos, there 'mid the scorn,
when nailed to a cross, all seemed lost,
except that God's love knows no cost.
The day of his rising is told
in Scripture with words that are bold.
Theotokos, what did she think,
that Mystery her life could link
all people with love-binding truth

---

3. Origin: Greek "theos" (god); Greek "-tokos" (bringing forth)

much stronger than ancestor Ruth?—
A love that goes where'er we go,
even when the way we do not know.
This love can save all humankind;
through Mary, God did it unbind.
The Mystery no words make true:
Love's Mystery depends on you.
This Mystery of love let be
God's Mystery of love in me.

Luke 1:30–31, "The angel said to her, 'Do not be afraid, Mary, for you have found favor with God. And now, you will conceive in your womb and bear a son, and you will name him Jesus.'"

11. Mary's Lullaby

While Mary sings a lullaby
as night enfolds the eastern sky,
    her son soon falls asleep.
She dreams of how he'll learn and grow,
his destiny she cannot know
    or that for him she'll weep.

She strokes his forehead with her hand
as wise men from a distant land
    seek one of royal birth;
but first come shepherds who were stirred
by angels' song on hillsides heard:
    "This Child brings peace on earth."

The shepherds hear the lullaby
the mother sings as they draw nigh
    to see the Holy Child:
"Sleep peacefully, sleep now in peace.
May love within your heart increase,
    in peace, be reconciled."

The wise men who have traveled far
to Bethlehem led by the star
    hear Mary's tuneful strain.
Gold, frankincense, and myrrh they bring—
the treasures that befit a king,
    the Prince of Peace's reign.

The lullaby that Mary sings
to every child life's meaning brings:
 "in peace, be reconciled."
If we will sing this lullaby,
then we will know the reason why
 he's born, this Holy Child.

Matthew 2:16, "When Herod saw that he had been tricked by the wise men, he was infuriated, and he sent and killed all the children in and around Bethlehem who were two years old or under, according to the time that he had learned from the wise men."

12. Mary, Joseph, Shepherds, Kings

Mary, Joseph, shepherds, kings,
while a heavenly chorus sings,
"Peace on earth and mercy mild,
God and sinners reconciled,"
learn of Israel's new-born King
though of different offspring.
He is born in David's line,
but is said to be divine.

Herod hears from far away
and decrees young babes to slay.
As the Wise Men come from far,
guided by the Bethl'hem star,
they bring gifts, so priceless, rare,
showing for the Child their care.
They know Herod's very wrong,
for they've heard the angels' song.

He'd demanded that they bring
details of the new-born king.
They go home another way,
Herod's anger to betray.
They refuse him a report;
they will not with him consort.
This child's fate would be quite grim,
should the Wise Men betray him!

Will this boy be called a king
without purple robes or ring?
His best friends will be the poor,
no delusions of grandeur.
A Messiah he will be
born oppressed folk to set free.
This is why the angels sing:
peace, goodwill this child will bring!

*Matthew 5:9, "Blessed are the peacemakers,
for they will be called children of God."*

13. Child of Peace

The idea of a God-made man,
    of God in human flesh,
as part of the Creator's plan,
    depicted in a crèche,
confuses some, to some gives hope,
    while others filled with awe
sense God's own view and widened scope
    of life by divine law.

Can there be order we can't grasp
    of One known as Divine?
Dare we the striking concept clasp:
    With God-made man align?
'Twas in a Child of peace God came
    a long-expected plan:
the life of love for all to frame
    in a small Child began.

It is the love the child made real
    as he grew to a man,
that filled the world with love to heal
    and sinfulness to ban.
The healing love of God's own Child
    still has much work to do,
for all, who are from loved exiled,
    need love from me, from you.

The God-Child's healing work of peace
    and love resides in us.
The hope that they will last, increase,
    makes sin superfluous.
If that's the case, we have to be
    those who make love and peace,
so that the love-exiled will see
    in them both have new lease.

Luke 2:16–18, 20, "So they [the shepherds] went with haste and found Mary and Joseph, and the child lying in a manger. When they saw this, they made known what had been told them about this child; and all who heard it were amazed at what the shepherds told them. . . . The shepherds returned, glorifying and praising God for all they had heard and seen, as it had been told them."

14. Christmas Time is Here at Last

Christmas greens and wreaths of red,
presents wrapped just as mom said,
crystal lights upon our tree,
Sarah Ann's wrapped gift for me,
garlands draped upon the door,
all foretell what is in store.
Special days that we await,
ones we all anticipate.
Colors, smells now tell us all,
It's time to sing "Deck the hall . . ."
Christmas time is finally here,
happiest time from year to year.
But it's much more than these things.
It's the time our church bell rings
calling us to come and hear
the same story heard each year
of a Child born in a stall
bringing peace and love to all.
This is why we decorate
in our homes and celebrate.
This Child's name Emmanuel
is the reason that we tell
of his birth and what it means,
"God with us" in many scenes.

Mary, Joseph, shepherds, kings,
as the angel chorus sings,
learn the truth of this Child's birth:
spread goodwill and peace on earth.

Luke 2:7, "And she gave birth to her firstborn son and wrapped him in bands of cloth and laid him in a manger, because there was no place for them in the inn."

15. God's Homeless Child

A homeless Child was born today,
his mother had no place to stay.
She found nowhere a welcome word;
"There is no room," was all she heard.
There was no place to lay his head,
a mother's arms his only bed.
There was no place to birth her boy,
yet angels hailed his birth with joy.

A homeless Child brings "peace on earth,"
the angels sang to greet his birth.
In homelessness God's love-born peace
is given life that will not cease.
When nearby shepherds heard the hymn,
they left their flocks for Bethlehem,
and there with wonder they beheld
the Child for whom the song had swelled.

How strange that wise men from afar
were guided by an eastern star
to cross the lonely desert wild
and journey to a homeless child.
Before the Child they humbly knelt,
a sense of royal awe they felt:
this homeless Prince of Peace will reign
with love for all that will not wane.

All homeless children here will find
a story that will bring to mind—
God chose a homeless Child to show
the lasting peace the world can know.
It's peace for those who have no home;
it's peace for those who idly roam;
it's peace for those who are at war;
it's peace for all, both near and far.

Matthew 1:21, "She will bear a son, and you are to name him Jesus, for he will save his people from their sins."

16. Who Was He?

A star with angels, shepherds, kings
    accompany a birth,
and still today a church bell rings,
    that's heard across the earth.

This bell and hosts of others sound
    the joyous angels' song,
to celebrate the world around
    this birth all the year long.

This Child in Bethlehem was born,
    where births happened each day.
Yet few folks sensed with a new morn
    who in a manger lay.

If he were just another boy,
    then why did angels sing,
and shepherds, even kings, find joy
    and to new hope would cling?

This Child was reason for new hope,
    he was God's song of peace,
who'd teach the world with wrong to cope
    through love's constant increase.

As he then grew, many a name
    on him was soon bestowed,
"The Prince of Peace" thence would proclaim
    the power that from him flowed.

Matthew 28:20, "And remember, I am with you always, to the end of the age."

17. Emmanuel—God with Us

"Always," Christ said, "I'll be with you."
Thus, we are not alone!
Faith only knows if this is true:
When "God with us" is known.

*Section 3*

After Christ Comes

Matthew 2:13–15, "Now after they had left, an angel of the Lord appeared to Joseph in a dream and said, 'Get up, take the child and his mother, and flee to Egypt, and remain there until I tell you; for Herod is about to search for the child, to destroy him.' Then Joseph got up, and took the child and his mother by night, and went to Egypt, and remained there until the death of Herod."

18. O, Jesus Child, Where are You?

After Jean Anouihl

O, Jesus Child, where are you? I see you are not there;
ox and ass alone surround a manger that is bare.
I see your mother, Mary, and Joseph hand in hand,
I see the stalwart wise men come from a foreign land.
And yet, I cannot find you: Where are you, Jesus Child?
"I'm in the hearts of poor folk, the wanton, the beguiled."

Now Mary is most anxious, you do not heed her call;
questioning the innkeeper, she searches in the stall.
Outside Joseph beckons you and combs the dark terrain.
The wise men fear your safety; their faces show the strain.
Now everyone is calling: Where are you, Jesus Child?
"I'm in the hearts of sick folk, even lonely souls turned wild."

The wise men have departed to eastern lands afar,
the shepherds on the hillside no longer see the star.
The night is cold and dreary—and vanished is the light,
and humankind is sighing: No Savior came that night.
Still wondering they question: Where are you, Jesus Child?
"I'm in the hearts of heathen with hope that's undefiled."

Matthew 2:6, "And you, Bethlehem, in the land of Judah, are by no means least among the rulers of Judah; for from you shall come a ruler who is to shepherd my people Israel."

19. Mourning for Bethlehem

Original poem by Phillip Brooks

O little town of Bethlehem, no longer still you lie. There is no deep and dreamless sleep for jets now fill the sky. Now in your dark streets standing are walls that shut out light; the hopes and fears of all the years aren't met in you tonight.	O little town of Bethlehem, how still we see thee lie; above thy deep and dreamless sleep the silent stars go by. Yet in thy dark streets shineth the everlasting light; the hopes and fears of all the years are met in thee tonight.
Though Christ was born of Mary, and gathered all above, no mortals sleep and soldiers keep no watch of wondering love. Though morning stars together proclaimed the holy birth, there is no song that we can sing, for there's no peace on earth.	For Christ is born of Mary, and gathered all above, while mortals sleep, the angels keep their watch of wondering love. O morning stars together, proclaim the holy birth, and praises sing to God the King, and peace to men on earth!
Not silently, not silently the wondrous gift is driven from human hearts though God imparts the blessings of his heaven. We hear the constant outburst of bombs and dying souls. Where is goodwill and peace on earth, for hate has no controls!	How silently, how silently, the wondrous gift is given; so God imparts to human hearts the blessings of his heaven. No ear may hear his coming, but in this world of sin, where meek souls will receive him, still the dear Christ enters in.

O holy Child of Bethlehem,
    descend to us we pray,
cast out our sin and enter in,
    be born in us today.
Instill the Christmas message
    of love, goodwill, and peace
in all on earth of every faith,
    that war and hatred cease.

O holy Child of Bethlehem,
    descend to us we pray,
cast out our sin and enter in,
    be born in us today.
We hear the Christmas angels
    the great glad tidings tell;
O come to us, abide with us,
    our Lord Emmanuel.

Luke 2:13–14, "And suddenly there was with the angel a multitude
of the heavenly host, praising God and saying,
'Glory to God in the highest heaven, and on earth peace, goodwill to all.'"[4]

20. The Christmas Bells of Bethlehem

> The Christmas bells of Bethlehem
>   ring once again for peace,
> while soldiers, as at Jesus' birth,
>   are "peace-making" police!
> "We'll keep the peace no matter what!"
>   Their oracle divine:
> "You think one little child brings peace?
>   Not so, it's our design!"
>
> The Christmas bells of Bethlehem
>   ring out "goodwill to all!"
> No matter what one's faith or creed,
>   goodwill creates no wall.
> What acts of goodwill shall we find
>   when bombs destroy a home,
> when children die of gunshot wounds,
>   and no one knows Shalom?
>
> The Christmas bells of Bethlehem
>   ring out, but who will hear?
> Their message is consistently
>   the same from year to year:
> "A Child brings peace, goodwill to earth."
>   Yet this seems hard to learn!
> A Child, goodwill, and lasting peace—
>   the world's yet to discern.

---

4. The New Revised Standard Version reads: "and on earth peace among those whom he favors!"

Ezekiel 13:9–11, "And you shall know that I am the Lord God. Because, in truth, they have misled my people, saying, 'Peace,' when there is no peace; and because, when the people build a wall, these prophets smear whitewash on it. Say to those who smear whitewash on it that it shall fall."

21. The Bethlehem Wall

There is no peace in Bethlehem,
    no matter what the angels sing.
The occupiers peace condemn,
    and build a wall, a doleful thing.

The Christians, Muslims they enclose,
    behind a town-encircling wall.
And peace, goodwill, as the wall shows,
    for coming years, it will forestall.

So, in the land where angels sang
    of peace on earth, goodwill to all,
and bells of peace so often rang,
    now Israel has built a wall.

What an illusion that a wall
    security and peace can bring.
Is it a foretaste of the fall
    that from imprisoned souls can spring?

But more important is the truth
    that peace, goodwill no boundaries know.
Who'll dare to teach this to the youth,
    who'll deal oppression a strong blow?

The Bethl'hem wall cannot contain
    the hope its citizens embrace.
Of peace, goodwill they'll sing again,
    the angels' song still has its place.

John 1:11, "He came to what was his own, and his own people did not accept him."

22. Questions and Answers

Was Christ Jesus born a stranger,
    neither prophet, priest, nor king?
Did they lay him in a manger?
    At his birth did angels sing?

There are those who ask in wonder,
    haunting questions plague us still.
Is truth's fabric rent asunder?
    Was his birth indeed God's will?

To these questions are there answers?
    Is there any certainty?
Does our doubt give birth to cancers
    that erode eternity?

The truth lies in Incarnation,
    divine love personified;
Love for all the true salvation,
    love for all for whom Christ died.

Valid answers lie in living,
    that's what Christ was born to show:
Truth is nothing without giving
    of yourself that love may grow.

Hence, trust the truth of Bethlehem,
    where love's Prophet, Priest, and King,
the source from which all truth must stem,
    love, the Christ Child's born to bring.

2 Corinthians 5:18–19, "All this is from God, who reconciled us to himself through Christ, and has given us the ministry of reconciliation; that is, in Christ God was reconciling the world to himself."

23. The Holy Grail of Christmas

Christmas came and went this year,
    so swiftly it passed by.
Though there was joy and some cheer,
    some folks were asking, Why?
No store-bought gifts could they share,
    no turkey could they eat.
Even so, they shared love and care,
    and Christmas was complete.

Can Christmas really take place
    when no gifts have been bought?
Can Christmas really take place
    when shopping is for naught?
Were sales as good as last year?
    Economists must know!
If not, there is the worst fear
    stock markets will be low.

Can this be what Christmas means
    to shop and buy each year?
If so, the poor are left out;
    this fact is surely clear.
Can there be a Christmas gift
    that never is for sale,
a gift every soul can lift?
    This gift's a Holy Grail.

It's not for sale in a shop
    no matter where you go.
So, let frantic shopping stop;
    this gift is not for show.
It is love, goodwill, and peace—
    The Holy Grail—a child,
Who's born these three to increase
    that *All* be reconciled.

Mark 8:36, "For what will it profit them to gain the whole world and forfeit their life?"

24. Corporate Christmas Cheer

With profits' gross lethality
    a threat at Christmas time,
Sales clerks decry frugality,
    for greed is in its prime.

Ostensibly Christmas is real,
    even merchants oft admit.
Most surely when the best sale deal
    is closed by sale-clerk grit.

One may believe most anything
    at Christmas-time each year:
As profits Jesus' story bring,
    the corporate world will cheer.

The story of an infant born,
    for whom the angels sing,
will increase sales for Christmas morn
    so, let the carols ring!

Psalms 40:3, "He put a new song in my mouth, a song of praise to our God."

25. Time to Cheer

The bells, the lights, and carol sings,
which every Christmas season brings,
the holly, ivy, Christmas trees,
the cookies, cakes that always please,
are but a sign that we need cheer
or they're just motions year on year.

But even routine cheer's not bad,
for few folks know the year you've had.
Still, Christmas never is routine;
each year there is a different scene:
Another child, grandchild is born,
another loved one that we mourn.

On Christmas morn, the church bells ring
reminding us that angels sing
of goodwill, peace throughout the earth;
both have new life through a Child's birth.
If there's good reason to rejoice,
then joyfully, shout, lend your voice.

It's time for humankind to cheer,
remove dark moods, the angry sneer.
Sing carols that proclaim goodwill
and louder yet proclaim the thrill
of peace that's possible right now;
the Christ Child's born to show us how.

Psalms 30:11–12, "You have turned my mourning into dancing;
you have taken off my sackcloth
and clothed me with joy,
so that my soul may praise you and not be silent.
O Lord my God, I will give thanks to you
forever.

26. Christmas Carols

When carolers at Christmas sing,
    O what an atmosphere!
The songs are not like anything
    one hears throughout the year.

When "Hark! the herald angels sing"
    resounds at Christmas time
The tune of Mendelssohn's the thing,
    for it fits Wesley's rhyme!

And then there is the lovely tune,
    that's sung for "Silent Night."
We sing it morning, evening, noon.
    It never becomes trite.

We love to sing the tune Greensleeves,
    in French sing "*Il est né*."
One carol, this thought with us leaves:
    that "Christ is born today!"

Section 4

Until Christ Comes

Ecclesiastes 1:9, "What has been is what will be,
and what has been done is what will be done;
there is nothing new under the sun."

Revelation 21:5, "And the one who was seated on the throne said,
'See, I am making all things new.' Also he said, 'Write this,
for these words are trustworthy and true.'"

27. Nothing New Under the Sun?

If nothing's new under the sun,
    as Hebrew Scriptures say,
how then can Jesus be the one
    who offers a new way?

"Behold, I will make all things new,"
    his bold and stunning claim,
but Koheleth,[5] the preacher, knew,
    he thought, things stay the same.

The Scriptures say God is the same,
    today and yesterday,
and Yahweh's the eternal name
    forever and for aye.

The constancy of the divine
    is Scripture's bold, stark view.
For this, is there from God a sign?
    If we God's thoughts but knew!

From Genesis to its last book
    the Bible has one theme:
to open human eyes to look
    at God's plan to redeem.

---

5. The Hebrew name of the biblical book otherwise known as Ecclesiastes.

But centuries came and centuries passed
    and humans could not see
their evil acts, turmoil amassed,
    had shaped their destiny.

So drastic was the earthly scene
    that even the divine
decided on a course pristine
    with hope hearts to incline.

Yes, something new under the sun
    omniscient God would plan,
the course of human history run:
    the advent of God-Man.

Yes, God old Koheleth defied
    and came to make things new,
and yet the old was not denied
    but seen from a new view.

The God-Man's name Emmanuel,
    "God with us" age to age,
makes new our lives—how long, how well—
    beyond the sacred page.

Luke 1:30, "The angel said to her, 'Do not be afraid, Mary, for you have found favor with God.'"

28. Who Is An Angel?

An angel tops a Christmas tree
    with stories it could tell
of hope and peace both yet to be
    on earth where people dwell.

An angel's other-worldly form
    of halos and of wings
reminds us it is not the norm
    of this world's earthly things.

Why then do angels trees adorn—
    because they sang one night
of goodwill to a world forlorn,
    of Peace-Child's guiding light?

When year by year an angel's there
    atop a Christmas tree,
it's more than decoration's flare:
    a sign what we're to be.

Be guardian angels, never cease
    benevolence, goodwill;
be watchful guardians of peace,
    for angels do no ill.

Each time the angel ornament's there,
    you'll see what you're to be,
an angel watchful everywhere,
    a peace, goodwill trustee.

Isaiah 11:6, "The wolf shall live with the lamb,
the leopard shall lie down with the kid,
the calf and the lion and fatling together,
and a little child shall lead them."

29. Whose Child Is This?

Whose child is this? I ask,
    a child you've never known?
Is it too great a task
    to love him as your own?
With food and shelter, tender care,
a healing touch, and clothes to wear—
with outstretched arms, will you be there?
Refrain: (after stanzas 1–6)
    Each child is God's child, yours, and mine—
    You are a gift of love divine.

Whose child is this? I see
    a child you've always known.
How strange it is to me—
    You've left her all alone!
In summer, autumn, winter, spring
you never thought—What shall I bring
to make her lonely spirit sing?

Whose child is this? who cries
    and stumbles in the street,
who trembles as he tries
    to walk on swollen feet?
Will no one take his hand and say,
"Come home with me where you may stay;
"I'll bathe your feet, the pain allay?"

"Whose child," I ask, "is this,
    who lives in wealth and ease,
who never feels a kiss,
    and parents cannot please."
Her angry words cry out, "I yearn
to find the love my heart would learn!"
Will she be forced such love to earn?

Whose child is this—black, red,
    white, yellow, bronze, or brown,
born without racists' dread
    or prejudicial frown?
Why teach a child hate, violence, greed?
And violate the Maker's creed:
Through love, God's love, the world is freed.

Once Jesus said, "Let all
    the children come to me."
If you would heed this call,
    like Jesus you must be.
Let all the children come to you:
the least, the last, vast numbers, few.
Our Savior bids you love them too.

Whose Child is this, I ask,
    who comes at Christmas time,
bringing a love to earth
    that makes all life sublime?
A Child in whom all children see
the kind of love that makes them free
to be what they are meant to be.
Refrain:
    This Child is God's Child, yours, and mine—
    Christ is a gift of love divine.

Psalms 39:12, "Hear my prayer, O Lord,
and give ear to my cry;
do not hold your peace at my tears."

30. We Pray for Peace

We pray for peace, we cry for peace,
    yet ravages of war
leave shattered lives without release
    in lands, both near and far.

Where children struggle to be fed
    without their parents' care.
Without a place to lay their head,
    they're trapped in dark despair.

Do we, God's creatures, have the will
    to do whate'er is just?
Will we oppose all war and fill
    hate's emptiness with trust?

O hear the angel's song of peace:
    "Goodwill to all on earth!"
Let hunger, hate, and violence cease
    and love enjoy new birth!

Matthew 1:23, "'Look, the virgin shall conceive and bear a son, and they shall name him Emmanuel,' which means, 'God with us.'"

31. Rethinking Christmas

Christmas is not an annual pause,
    though that is useful too,
if pausing makes you think its cause
    is worth rethinking through.

The cause we're told: there was a need
    on earth for love and peace.
the world was overcome with greed.
    How then could they increase?

The increase came with a Child's birth
    though some still think untrue.
How could a Child bring peace on earth?
    None knew until he grew.

Emmanuel was this Child's name
    but why was he named this?
"God with us," as he grew became
    a name not to dismiss.

Emmanuel personified,
    Peace/Love in deed and word,
he taught and lived them as a guide
    till strife/hate seemed absurd.

So, if we pause and do rethink
    what Christmas for us means,
perhaps we'll ask if we're in sync
    with Peace/Love in our genes!

*2 Corinthians 4:18, "We look not at what things can be seen but at what
cannot be seen; for what can be seen is temporary,
but what cannot be seen is eternal."*

32. Seeing the Unseen

Such words as wonder, glorious, awe
are uttered when something I saw
so moved my heart and soul with joy
that both an inner thrill deploy?

Can this be true, if I don't see
the wonder that is meant for me?
The unseen can evoke such awe.
What? Something that I never saw?

How does the heart know what is real?
Is awe enough for truth's appeal?
I see no God and yet believe,
but not so I my fears relieve.

If reason's only what I seek
with logic's often added tweak,
then I am truly at a loss—
the unexplained's an albatross.

Faith stands within itself to view:
the unexplained is given its due.
"Example, Christmas," I should say,
"reveals the most transforming day."

We read a story, sing then songs
that God upon the earth belongs.
But love divine personified
by humans soon is crucified.

Yet love like this lives on, that's sure,
for ages, Scriptures us assure;
the prophets, priests, and sages past
say, "Love the least, the lost, the last."

This is the love that Christmas brings
even though I see no shepherds, kings.
I see no Savior born anew,
lest selfless love daily I view.

Luke 6:31, "Do to others as you would have them do to you."

Matthew 25:45, "Truly, I tell you, just as you did not do it to one of the least of these, you did not do it to me."

33. Christmas Joy

The holidays are hard to bear
for those under the weight of care.
Though some folks cheer, and others sing,
some simply have no joy to bring.
A mother's sick, a father dies,
an orphan child just sits and cries.
While sadness is found everywhere,
can Christmas be a time to share?

As difficult as it may be,
no day on earth concerns just me.
For every one of my own foils
the happiness of life recoils.
As someone dies, a child is born,
a sick child's healed on a new morn.
So, where there's sadness, there is hope,
though for it some folks daily grope.

Think first of others and their needs,
and though your heart with anguish bleeds,
you'll find there's solace in the thought
that you're not in self-pity caught.
This Christmas cannot pain remove,
but there is something it can prove:
A love-born Child gives hope to all,
a love-born Child birthed in a stall.

Psalms 98:4, "Make a joyful noise to the Lord, all the earth; break forth into joyous song and sing praises."

34. Joy

Why is a holiday so hard?
I just received a lovely card.
It says there's joy that's all around,
but where, oh where can it be found?
If joy is just a written word,
a word that's read but never heard,
a word not spoken, given voice,
the silence is by one's own choice.
Joy must be lived, personified.
The gift of joy one should not hide.
Joy heals the saddest broken heart.
Joy's to be lived with each day's start.
It won't be then a word you read,
It will express just what you need!

Isaiah 9:6, "For a child has been born for us,
a son given to us;
authority rests upon his shoulders;
and he is named
Wonderful Counselor, Mighty God,
Everlasting Father, Prince of Peace."

35. A Single Bell

I heard a bell on Christmas Day,
uncertain what it had to say.
Our church was gone, by bombs destroyed;
the place it stood was empty, void.
Alone the tower with its bell
was left, next to an old hotel.
A young boy then the bell rope took,
and rang the bell till houses shook.
No one expected such a sound,
for scarce a soul was to be found.
And yet, that day I heard it ring;
what joy it did to my heart bring!
The church had vanished, still I heard
a bell ring out the Christmas word:
Peace, peace, the bell's loud, clarion call.
A single bell had said it all.

Joel 2:28, "Then afterward
I will pour out my spirit on all flesh;
your sons and your daughters shall prophesy,
your old men shall dream dreams,
and your young men shall see visions."

36. No Christmas is the Same

Were I to have a Christmas thought
    besides the gifts and mistletoe,
it would not be of what I'd bought,
    but of my family years ago.

Oh, how we laughed, sang Christmas songs,
    and round a table shared a feast.
We knew where every heart belongs
    from grandma to the very least.

The times have changed, and grandma's gone
    and brand-new babies have been born,
but still the family carries on,
    the young grow older, some more worn.

Our family changes year by year:
    new children born, new grandmas made,
new Christmas recipes appear,
    new loves the young and old pervade.

That's why no Christmas is the same
    as one remembered from the past.
Traditions old and new we claim,
    and thus, our family's die is cast.

Proverbs 10:7, "The memory of the righteous is a blessing."

37. Christmas Memories

Though Christmas time is filled with life,
    it calls to mind mortality:
the absence of a husband, wife
    embraced now by eternity.
They loved the joys of Christmas time,
    the decorations, carol sings,
the melodies and texts that rhyme,
    the family closeness Christmas brings.

I know they'd want us all to thank
    each family member, every friend
with grateful words, with words quite frank,
    for Christmas joys shared without end.
Since Christmas is about new birth,
    of them let memories be reborn;
and as we sing of peace on earth,
    remember them on Christmas morn.

Lamentations 3:21–22, "But this I call to mind, and therefore I have hope: The steadfast love of the Lord never ceases, his mercies never come to an end."

38. Too Late for Peace, Goodwill?

There was a time that Christmas charm
could evil in the world disarm.
That's what I thought as a young boy,
for Christmas time was filled with joy.
I saw a lovely Christmas tree
and heard my friends sing merrily
the carols' words "goodwill" and "peace,"
that would throughout the world increase.
And yet, the world was then at war,
at five years, I knew not what for.
My friends sang, "peace and mercy mild,"
which rhymed with the word "reconciled."
At five years old, I did not know
the world in my life would not show
it understood what these words meant,
for still it was on war hell-bent.
When I was grown, I came to see
that Christmas must at first change me.
The message of that Christmas night:
a new-born Child brings love and light
into a world that is forlorn
is why a God-Child would be born.
This message still is up-to-date,
yet, every year it seems too late:
too late to make peace where there's hate,
too late for goodwill to create.
But still the carols we will sing
with hope that Christmas peace will bring.

Jeremiah 6:14, "They have treated the wound of my people carelessly,
saying, 'Peace, peace,'
when there is no peace."

39. If Christmas Comes

If Christmas comes and there's no peace
    or comes without goodwill,
did angels sing to no avail
    to shepherds on a hill?
If Wise Men traveled from the East
    with gifts for royalty,
and found no newborn King of kings,
    was it futility?

If there's no reign of peace on earth,
    if goodwill yields to hate,
can we be sure a Savior came?
    Must we then longer wait?
Illusion is it now to trust
    that hearts can yet be changed,
goodwill and peace somehow transform
    those evil has estranged?

These questions haunt me on the night
    the Savior Christ was born.
I yearn, I yearn answers to find,
    lest I of hope be shorn.
In quietness, I realize
    the answers are within.
In others, I will find no peace,
    in me it must begin.

Goodwill must win my every thought,
    and kindness be my guide;
concern for others uttermost,
    all evil deeds decried.
Each year the angels' song is sung
    as at the Savior's birth,
that peace and goodwill have the chance
    to spread throughout the earth.

Micah 5:2, 4–5, "But you, O Bethlehem of Ephrathah,
who are one of the little clans of Judah,
from you shall come forth for me
one who is to rule in Israel, . . .
he shall be great
to the ends of the earth;
and he shall be the one of peace."

40. Give Peace, Goodwill New Birth

Around Christ's birthplace Bethlehem
    there's now a city wall.
Will this the Christmas song condemn
    as obsolete for all?
Goodwill and peace aren't for a few
    on one side of the wall.
The message is forever new:
    a universal call!

The truth is every human soul
    deserves goodwill and peace;
this Christmas message may console,
    yet unjust acts increase.
What does the Christmas message say?
    Opinions come and go.
For some it's just another day
    of rain or winter snow.

You may not think a Christ Child came
    with lofty goals like these.
But even so, we are to blame
    if we self-will appease.
"Peace on the earth, good will to all,"
    the angel chorus sings,
and both transcend the Bethl'hem wall:
    the gift each Christmas brings.

Oh yes, I know thousands of deeds
    of goodwill find their way
to places of grave human needs,
    and words of peace we say.
We cannot make the angels' song
    reality on earth
unless we for our whole lives long
    give peace, goodwill new birth.

www.ingramcontent.com/pod-product-compliance
Lightning Source LLC
Chambersburg PA
CBHW071742040426
42446CB00012B/2444